MW00875397

THE CREATOR'S TOY CHEST

© 2018 by Creator's Toy Chest LLC

Published by Baker Books
A division of Baker Publishing Group
PO Box 6287, Grand Rapids, MI 49516-6287
www.bakerbooks.com

First Edition

Printed in the United States of America

Library of Congress Cataloging-in-Publication Data
Names: Blair, Brett, author. | Koenig, James, illustrator.
Title: Creator's toy chest : Creation's story / Brett Blair ; illustrated by James Koenig.
Description: First edition. | Grand Rapids : Baker Publishing Group, 2018. | Summary: From a chaotic toy chest, God brings order as he creates the earth and what dwells there.
Identifiers: LCCN 2017052844 | ISBN 9780801017186 (cloth)
Subjects: | CYAC: Creation—Fiction. | God (Christianity)—Fiction.
Classification: LCC PZ8.3.B575 Cr 2018 | DDC [E]—dc23
LC record available at https://lccn.loc.gov/2017052844

Published in association with the literary agency D.C. Jacobson & Associates, an Author Management Company, www.dcjacobson.com.

18   19   20   21   22   23   24   7   6   5   4   3   2   1

THE CREATOR'S TOY CHEST

• Creation's Story •

Brett Blair

Illustrated by James Koenig

BakerBooks

a division of Baker Publishing Group
Grand Rapids, Michigan

• • •

To Cyndi

My Love

• • •

In the beginning, there was nothing at all.
Nothing was short and nothing was tall.
Nothing was big and nothing was small.
In the beginning, there was nothing at all.

Then, nothing was something.
It was something to see!
God said a small word.
He said, "Let it BE."

This BE was big.
    BE echoed and rang.
Into BEing, all things sprang.

When the earth was formed and the heavens,
In this ancient of stories: the Days of Seven.

No one could see
in the dark of the night.
So God entered the room,
turned on the light.

8

The light did help, but, oh, what a mess.
It looked like a chaotic Creator's toy chest.
Look north, look south, look east, look west.
The earth needed order, but what to do next?

And then God spoke.
He calmed wild oceans with blankets of sky,
Lifted the clouds so water could fly.

It warmed. It cooled. It rained. It snowed.
It stormed. It shined. It dried. It glowed.
The light so bright. The sky so grand.

But in a watery wet world, there's no place to stand.

So with rocks, clay, dirt, and sand, in loving hands

He mixed and folded, shaped and molded the land.

Then the world's first Gardener kneeled on one knee,
Dug up the dirt, and planted the tree.

Bushes, flowers, grass, and reeds,
Veggies, fruits, nuts, and seeds.

Mango, apple, celery, onion,
Kiwi, cocoa, peanut, pumpkin.

The Lord produced a tremendous scene,
Filling the world with splendiferous green.

Then with great care God worked on his math,
Planned the heavens on an infinity graph.

$$r = \frac{p}{1 + \varepsilon \cos \theta}$$

f2

A2

a2

A1

a1

$$\frac{dA}{dt} = \frac{1}{2} r^2 \frac{d\theta}{dt}$$

Thousands, millions, billions, and trillions.
Dare I now say, he created zillions?

$$\frac{P^2}{a^3} = \frac{4\pi^2}{G(M+m)} \approx \frac{4\pi^2}{GM}$$

Galaxies here, galaxies there,
Planets and stars and moons everywhere.
The sky lit up with the sun and the moon.
The Father gave us a cozy warm room.

And then God paused, took a deep breath,
And deep down within his Creator's toy chest
Blew big bubbles where coral colors swirl,
A bowl of fish the size of the world.

Catfish, lionfish, sailfish, swordfish.
Clownfish, blowfish, starfish, goldfish.

He filled rivers,
lakes, oceans, and skies
With creatures of every
shape, strength, color, and size.

Woodpecker, kingfisher, albatross, dipper.
Flamingo, cockatoo, hummingbird, skimmer.

He finished this work of feather and fin
By blessing these creatures: "Be fruitful, begin."

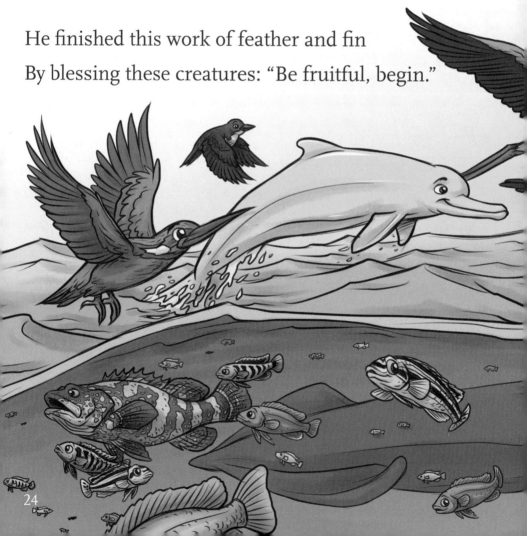

"Now it is time," God said on the sixth day,

"For the short to be short,
The tall to be tall,
The big to be big,
The small to be small."

Crawlers, climbers,
jumpers, runners.
Barkers, bleaters,
trumpers, grunters.

27

With a satisfied heart, God finished his quest
By searching deep down in the Creator's toy chest.
Finding nothing to use for the final plan,
In the image of God, he created man.

God sat down and rummaged through the toy chest.
Checking the math on the infinity graph,
It all added up. He was finished. All done.
And with the pride of a father and the love of a mom,
God sang to the heavens this very first psalm:

"Good is the short.
Good is the tall.
Good is the big.
Good is the small."

"Let us rest," God said, "and enjoy all this good.
Our work here is done. Rest, we all should."

So the days came to an end,
When the Creator created
and creatures said, "Amen!"

Now late at night when stars twinkle in heaven,
Remember the toy chest
and the days of seven.